IMAGES OF WAR
ROMMEL'S ARMY IN THE DESERT

IMAGES OF WAR
ROMMEL'S ARMY IN THE DESERT

ALISTAIR SMITH

Pen & Sword
MILITARY

First published in Great Britain in 2013 by
PEN & SWORD MILITARY
an imprint of
Pen & Sword Books Ltd,
47 Church Street, Barnsley,
South Yorkshire.
S70 2AS

ISBN 978-1-84884-807-8

A CIP catalogue record for this book is available
from the British Library

Typeset by Mac Style, Beverley, East Yorkshire
Printed and bound by CPI Group (UK) Ltd, Croydon, CR0 4YY

Pen & Sword Books Ltd incorporates the imprints of
Pen & Sword Books Ltd incorporates the Imprints of Pen & Sword Aviation,
Pen & Sword Family History, Pen & Sword Maritime, Pen & Sword Military, Pen & Sword
Discovery, Wharncliffe Local History, Wharncliffe True Crime, Wharncliffe Transport,
Pen & Sword Select, Pen & Sword Military Classics, Leo Cooper, The Praetorian Press,
Remember When, Seaforth Publishing and Frontline Publishing

For a complete list of Pen & Sword titles please contact:
PEN & SWORD BOOKS LIMITED
47 Church Street, Barnsley, South Yorkshire, S70 2AS, England.
E-mail: enquiries@pen-and-sword.co.uk
Website: www.pen-and-sword.co.uk

Contents

Introduction

When German General Rommel and his lead elements of what would become the Afrika Korps landed in Libya in February 1941 nobody could foresee the legendary status they would achieve.

For some they were the perfect desert army. They were a lean, hard-hitting combination of units. Always outnumbered by their Italian allies in the desert, they were to perform absolute miracles on a tiny budget and resources.

North Africa, although a crucial theatre of the war, never achieved the importance of mainland Europe. For two years, however, it gave Britain and the Commonwealth and, later, the Americans, an opportunity to fight Germany.

The Afrika Korps had been sent to North Africa to bolster the faltering Italians. If Germany's ally was decisively defeated in North Africa, the Allies would menace the so-called 'soft belly of Europe'. They could strike against Germany or Italy against Greece to the east, to the coast of southern France in the west.

The North African campaign was fought over one of the most inhospitable environments of the war. The very ground itself was hostile and unyielding. For the Afrika Korps, often outnumbered and out-gunned, they managed to drive the Allies to the very gates of Egypt. Rommel and his Afrika Korps were only finally undone by their defeat at the hands of Montgomery at El Alamein and the subsequent Allied landings to their rear in Tunisia.

This collection of photographs is taken from three albums belonging to members of the much vaunted Afrika Korps. For the first time the daily realities of the North African campaign can be seen from a German point of view. With numerous photographs of vehicles and the rigours of the campaign the combined collection paints a portrait of the rugged and dangerous conditions, as well as the harsh and brutal nature of desert warfare. The photographic albums are owned by James Payne, who runs 'Through Their Eyes', an unrivalled collection of historic wartime photographs. If readers wish to obtain their own high resolution copies of these photographs then they should contact James at www.throughtheireyes2.co.uk.

In selecting the various shots from a combined collection of over 600, it proved challenging to choose truly representative images. Like many wartime photographic albums, the sadness lies in the fact that the photographers' names are completely unknown. No trace of identification is included in the original albums. Very few of the photographs have a date, location, or identify those being pictured. Whilst impeded by this lack of information it is an opportunity to look at the photographs with fresh eyes and not to be swayed by any passing caption or comment. It makes these images more innocent and representative of daily life and reality.

Undoubtedly, like so many British and Commonwealth troops that fought in North Africa, the sight of the barren deserts for the first time for individuals who had been born and raised in the relative lush green of northern Europe must have been a huge shock.

Casualty figures are confused for the Afrika Korps. Technically speaking some German units were not Afrika Korps formations at all. On a conservative level the Germans are thought to have lost some 18,500 men killed. In addition to this nearly 3,500 were posted as missing in action and a further 130,000 were taken as prisoners of war. Their Italian allies of course lost huge numbers of men and materials too. It has been estimated that over 22,000 Italians were killed and at least 340,000 taken prisoner. In all, the war was ruinous in terms of material. Individual figures are difficult to unravel, but between Germany and Italy they lost some 800 aircraft, over 6,000 artillery pieces, 2,500 tanks and a further 70,000 vehicles. Although many of these were destroyed a large number were either captured by the Allies or abandoned due to mechanical failure, or simply because they had run out of fuel.

These photographs seek to chronicle the events that took place between February 1941, with the arrival of the Germans in North Africa, and the final surrender on 13 May 1943.

The harsh reality of death in the desert; German soldiers are digging graves in the sand. It would appear that a burial has just taken place and that the grave is being filled in. Unfortunately it is not possible to read any of the names on the crosses, or to pinpoint the location of this photograph.

Chapter 1

Operation Sonnenblume

On 10 June 1940 Italy declared war on Britain and France. The Italian plan was simple and cynical; France was on her knees and Britain was sorely stretched. The Italians hoped to seize French Colonial possessions in North Africa, take the Alps and the area around Nice. At the same time they would try to grab Egypt and to expand their East African possessions at the expense of the French and the British.

Italy, however, was woefully unprepared for war. British troops in Egypt were undermanned and under-equipped. They were told to defend Egypt but not to make any provocative moves against the Italians. In fact they did, in the form of raids. British troops crossed into Libya, ambushed Italian motorized transport and seized the forts of Capuzzo and Maddalena.

Mussolini was livid and ordered a full-scale assault on the British in Egypt. This finally got underway in mid-September 1940. Five Italian divisions crossed the border; they were spearheaded by 200 tanks. The Italians seized Sollum and then, two days later and some 60 miles further into Egypt, they took Sidi Barrani.

Inexplicably, the Italian forces under Marshal Graziani then stopped and began to dig in. Incredible as it may seem, in the new, fluid Blitzkrieg war of the 1940s, the Italians were prepared to simply sit and consolidate their gains. Had the Italians continued the war in North Africa at this point it would have been over. The British simply lacked the men and resources to withstand a determined assault. Mussolini was, understandably, angry, frustrated and adamant that the offensive should resume. Graziani relented and planned to attack again in October. In the end he changed his mind and continued to fortify his gains. Graziani planned to leave considerable numbers of troops in their fortified camps and use the Italian 10th Army to launch the new offensive.

In fact it was the British under Wavell that launched the offensive. The British and Commonwealth troops, although weakened by the siphoning off of forces to bolster the Greeks against the Italians on the European mainland, attacked in December 1940. Had the Italians struck first they would have found an ill-prepared and much depleted British Army in Egypt. Who knows, they could have broken through and launched assaults deep into the Middle East. This would have denied Britain the Suez Canal and would have made it incredibly difficult for the British to use reinforcements from India.

On 9 December 1940 the Royal Navy began shelling Sidi Barrani and Maktila. Spearheading the ground attack was the Indian 4th Division. Supported by tanks, the Commonwealth troops took the forts at Nibeiwa and Tummar. It was a costly victory, with nearly fifty British tanks succumbing to Italian anti-tank guns.

Nonetheless, Wavell's men pressed on. The British 7th Armoured took Sofafi and Rabia but the weakness of the deep prongs allowed many Italians to break out to the west. By the time the British had reached Bardia they had scooped up around 38,000 prisoners, over 200 artillery pieces and around seventy tanks. By 21 December the Italians were desperately hanging on to Bardia. They withstood assaults from Australian troops for two weeks before exhaustion, low ammunition and continual bombardment forced a surrender.

By early January 1941 the British had overrun Tobruk. The Italian 10th Army had been shattered and 100,000 had been taken prisoner. At times the Italians had stubbornly fought back, such as at Derna, but all efforts had failed. The British 7th Armoured was now just 70 miles from Benghazi itself.

In the nick of time General Valentino Babini, in Libya, received the help he so badly needed. A new, special armoured brigade called the Brigata Corazzato Speciale, armed with Italian tanks and specialist anti-tank infantry, blunted the British armoured thrusts. Effectively, this turned the tide once again. On 24 January the unit knocked out more than twenty Matilda tanks.

On the verge of being annihilated the Italians were now fighting back. The British also were facing increased numbers of Italian aircraft. Regardless of the slowly improving fortunes of the Italians in North Africa, Hitler was induced to get involved. In fact it seemed like a perfect opportunity and a remote enough theatre to slowly bleed Britain to death. If he could induce them to divert material to North Africa they would not be in a position to interfere with his other plans, notably his impending invasion of Russia.

Hitler did not propose to flood the North African theatre with troops and equipment. But he needed someone who could equip themselves, someone who was daring and someone who was prepared to take the risks. He chose Erwin Rommel.

The Afrika Korps began arriving at Tripoli on 12 February 1941. The lead elements consisted of one Panzer division and a light division. It was incredibly well timed; at the beginning of February the British had knocked out eighty Italian tanks and captured seven senior officers at Benghazi. A day later 20,000 troops, 120 tanks and 200 artillery pieces had been captured by Wavell. Despite the Italian disasters, Rommel immediately went on the offensive and over the course of the next two months he took back everything that Wavell and his troops had taken from the Italians. Rommel and his Afrika Korps were to prove to be a thorn in the side of the Allied efforts for over two years, but first it would be a long road to Egypt.

This chapter is called Operation Sonnenblume, or 'sunflower' and due to the nature of the photographs, which are almost tourist-like, it would appear that the photographer had never driven along these roads before, so it must be assumed that they were involved in the first German deployment in the spring of 1941.

German truck drivers take a rest on the road east in this photograph. The most commonly used German truck was the Opel Blitz, which was actually manufactured between around 1930 and 1975. The most frequently used version during the Second World War was a 3tonner. It was a truly multipurpose vehicle; as a supply truck both the sides and back were designed to drop down. As a personnel carrier benches were fitted along the length of the back of the truck and only the rear could be opened. The most common version was the S model, which saw more than 100,000 units produced. There were 25,000 of the A model produced from 1940. What was particularly good about the Opel Blitz was that it was capable of carrying a relatively heavy load compared to its weight, it was extremely reliable and Germany had set up an extremely efficient spare parts supply network.

This is a view across the scrub from the front of an Opel Blitz, looking towards more trucks parked in the distance. When the first German troops arrived in North Africa in February 1941 they were immediately sent to the front line, which was then in the port of Sirte. The new arrivals consisted of the 5th Light Division. It was a Panzer heavy unit that had been loaded onto Italian cargo ships at Naples. The other division was the 15th Panzer, which was a relatively newly created unit. The 8th Panzer Regiment, consisting of some 146 tanks, arrived in three separate convoys between the end of April and the beginning of May 1941. The new German arrivals appeared in North Africa towards the end of the British offensive codenamed Operation *Compass*. This had seen British troops stopping just short of total victory. Instrumental in the developing situation that had allowed the Germans to land in North Africa was the crippling of HMS *Illustrious*. This had been seriously damaged by Italian dive bombers on 11 January 1941. Without the aircraft carrier's aircraft and support the German units were able to slip across the Mediterranean.

This photograph is marked as having been taken at Derna. During Operation *Compass* Derna had seen some heavy fighting. British troops had taken Tobruk and with it its 17,000-manned garrison. The Italians had put together the Special Armoured Brigade, which was specifically created as an anti-tank unit. On 24 January lead elements of the British 4th Armoured Brigade were engaged by the new Italian unit on the Derna to Mechili track. The Italians lost nine tanks and the British seven. The day after, at Derna airfield, the same Italian unit was part of a series of counterattacks. On 27 January the Australians came under a determined assault by around 1,000 Italian infantry and on the same day the British 6th Cavalry Regiment was ambushed by this Italian unit, but the advance of other British units threatened the Italians with being cut off and they pulled back under cover of darkness on 28 January. Derna had been captured on 26 January.

A line of German trucks are seen here, trying to make progress along a sandy track in the desert. The angles of the vehicles show the treacherous nature of the soft and shifting sands of the desert. The Opel Blitz was a simple and robust design. In terms of its deployment in the desert it was probably ideal because it exerted a low ground pressure due to its low unladen weight. Nonetheless, as we can see from this photograph, loaded or unloaded the desert presented the drivers with unique challenges.

This photograph is captioned Beute, which simply means 'trophy'. The Germans were not averse to using captured enemy vehicles and pressing them into action. In fact many French tanks that had been captured as early as May 1940 were to face Shermans and Churchills in Normandy in 1944. This photograph would appear to feature a Marmon-Herrington armoured car. It was one of the most commonly used vehicles in British armoured car units until at least 1942. In fact there were around 1,200 of them in service. The armoured car was still seen as late as May 1943 and some units even used them in Italy. The British would later also use them in Malaya and the South Africans were particularly keen on the vehicles, with 4,500 of them. The vehicle itself came from an American car manufacturer known as the Marmon Car Company. In the early 1930s a Colonel Arthur Herrington joined the company as an engineer and they began developing military vehicles. In addition to the British and South Africans using the vehicle they were also used by New Zealanders and the Free Greeks, French and Poles. Understandably, given the fluid nature of the desert warfare, a considerable number of them were captured by the Germans, who were all too happy to press them into service.

This snatched photograph was taken from the back of a moving truck and appears to show the overturned body of an abandoned vehicle. Although it is difficult to tell this could easily be an abandoned Matilda tank, although it is more likely to be an Italian medium tank, possibly the M11/39. This particular tank was based on the Vickers 6ton tank and had a limited traverse 37mm gun. In early encounters with British lighter tanks it was pretty successful but when faced with typical British cruiser tanks or infantry tanks such as the A9, A10, A13 and Matilda it was seriously outclassed. The M11/39 was involved in the Italian invasion of Egypt in September 1940 and it certainly saw service during Operation *Compass*. The Italians lost large numbers of the tanks during this phase of the North African campaign. Many were knocked out or immobilized and a huge number of them were simply captured because they could not cope with the heavy armour of the Matilda tanks. Like the Germans, the British were only too happy to use foreign vehicles and in fact the 6th Australian Division Cavalry Regiment painted white kangaroos on the sides of the captured M11/39s during the siege of Tobruk from April 1941. They continued to use them until they ran out of fuel and then set off detonation charges to stop them falling back into the hands of their previous owners.

This photograph was probably taken at dusk or at dawn on the coastal road running east towards Egypt. In the distance we can see a number of trucks parked up and tents have been erected. The coast road would prove to be incredibly valuable as a main arterial route to supply the Afrika Korps. At virtually no time during the course of the war in North Africa was the Mediterranean safe for either Italian or German vessels. This meant that any supplies that did manage to run the gauntlet of the Royal Navy had often to be driven hundreds of miles along the coastal road to the front lines. Rommel and his Afrika Korps would always find themselves short of materials and supplies. When he captured Tobruk in June 1942 the windfall from the captured British supplies sustained him for some time, but this was only a temporary respite. Although the job of ferrying supplies up and down the coast road by truck was not a romantic occupation, it was absolutely vital to sustain the Afrika Korps.

Trucks are moving into an oasis here. For centuries traders and others had passed through the deserts of North Africa. This is only made possible by the oases, but even along the coast in the north trucks would have to drive sometimes for days before reaching a new oasis. Crossing the desert without them would have been impossible. It was not necessarily the temperature, but the dryness that was the problem. The Sahara is the largest desert on the earth and on average just 3 inches of rain fall in a year. This is what made the oasis so important, as in some regions although it may rain on one day the rain may not return for several years.

This photograph would appear to have been taken in Libya, given the more sophisticated infrastructure. Note the tarmac road, the warning bollards along the side of the road and the telephone cables stretching out into the distance along the roadside. Also note the comparative lush vegetation. The Italians had taken Libya from the Ottomans in 1912 and had undergone enormous development in a relatively short period of time. Mussolini had visited Libya in 1937. Initially the Italians were reticent about Libyans joining their military but they reformed their policy in 1939 and in March 1940 over 30,000 native Libyans were drafted into two divisions. They took part in the Italian offensive against Egypt. There were considerable numbers of Italians in Libya and they tended to focus on the more temperate coastal areas. By 1940 around 12 per cent of the population was Italian, roughly 110,000. Most of them lived either in Tripoli or Benghazi. The Italian government was keen for Libya to be properly colonized and they built almost thirty new villages for some 20,000 Italian farmers in 1938.

This is a fascinating photograph of what appears to be an Italian colonial fort. Note the radio mast fixed to the watchtower. Unfortunately it has not been possible to identify this fort, but the Italians made extensive use of forts. Perhaps the most famous in Libya was Fort Capuzzo. This was built close to the Libyan border with Egypt and close to what was known as the Frontier Wire. This wire ran nearly 170 miles from El Ramleh on the coast all the way to Jaghbub, a remote desert oasis in the eastern Libyan Desert. Fort Capuzzo had been captured by the 11th Hussars a few days after Italy had declared war against Britain in June 1940. The fort was recaptured by the Italian 1st Blackshirt Division, who stormed on towards Sidi Barrani. The British recaptured it again in December 1940, Rommel took it back in April 1941, and the British grabbed it in the May and then lost it until it was taken by the New Zealanders in November 1941. It fell into German hands again after the Battle of Gazala, which took place between May and June 1942 and then it permanently fell into Allied control after the second battle of El Alamein, fought between October and November 1942.

There is a good deal of speculation about this photograph which appears to feature unidentified British troops. The likelihood is that this is a captured photograph. In the background we can see a British staff car, probably an Austin. The featuring of captured photographs in German war albums was quite commonplace. Here we can see British soldiers cleaning out their mess tins, probably in Libya. The Italians had poured an enormous amount of resources into the infrastructure of Libya. They planned towns, wrought irrigation miracles and managed to set up plantations in the most adverse of conditions. The Italians were also instrumental in building what was known as the Litoranea, which was the Egypt to Tunisia coastal highway. Italian Libya consisted of four provinces; Tripoli, Misurata, Benghazi and Derna and it became the nineteenth region of metropolitan Italy. The Italians had transformed the country but many of the locals were forced to give up their old way of life in return for employment. The Italians built aqueducts, roads, houses, barracks, military stores and new civic centres.

This fascinating photograph shows a bewildering selection of headgear as mass catering takes place on implausibly long tables with benches alongside a bell tent city. It is not obvious where this photograph was taken but some of the men, particularly those to the rear of the photograph, appear to be wearing the German tropical helmet. This was of a lightweight canvas construction and it had a broad rim in order to protect the wearer from the sun. The dome at the top was fitted with four small holes or arches to encourage the circulation of air. On the sides of the helmet were shields; one showed the national colours whilst the second showed the army eagle. These shields were fitted to the canvas by metal prongs. They would often be worn with desert goggles, which were made of brown rubber and had plastic lenses. This was in fact a modern version of the sun hat that the Germans had worn during the First World War. Essentially it was pretty much the same design. Inside the dome was a red fabric and there was a leather sweat band around the bottom of the dome on the inside. The manufacturer's logo was often stamped into the sweat band. The helmet had a green leather chinstrap.

A second fascinating captured British photograph which was included in the German war album. In the early war years, some British troops were still wearing 1897 vintage pattern khaki drill service dress. Gradually this was phased out. In fact as late as 1943 some units in India were actually issued with this kit. Shorts were fairly common, they did not have the Field Dressing Pocket. The troops here appear to be wearing 1937 pattern webbing. Most interesting is the helmet. This was known as the Wolseley Pattern Pith Helmet, although in India it was called the Cawnpore helmet. In the period 1941–43 the pith helmet was largely discarded in North Africa, so too was the khaki drill service dress. Bush shirts became popular; this was adopted as the walking out dress for most ranks, some wore them in battle.

German units arriving in North Africa would only be reissued with North African gear as and when this became available. The truck drivers were not, of course, front line troops. However they would have been required to carry out routine security duties, including posting guard on their encampments. They would also be expected to be able to fend for themselves to a large extent.

Chapter 2

Towards the Front

The term Afrika Korps is somewhat confusing. It is generally used as a generic term to describe the German units that were deployed in North Africa. Technically speaking, the better description is Panzer Army Afrika. This actually consisted of a pair of armoured divisions, two motorised divisions and three infantry divisions that were all German. In addition to this there were eight Italian divisions and the Folgore Italian Parachute Division. Over the period February 1941 to May 1943 several other smaller units were attached to the main army.

When Rommel and the lead elements of the German force arrived between February and March 1941 the Italians had been pushed back hundreds of miles. The first German unit to arrive was the 5th Light Division. Essentially it was an ad hoc unit and comprised of elements of the 3rd Panzer Division. The formation was renamed in mid-February 1941 and placed under the command of General-Major Johannes Streich. He had commanded the 15th Panzer Regiment in France in 1940. The units began arriving in Tripoli, but the last elements did not arrive until mid-March, so they missed Rommel's first offensive.

To begin with the 5th Light was undermanned and under-resourced and had around 130 serviceable tanks. Being undermanned was a constant issue for elements of the Afrika Korps; they always seemed to be the last in line for reinforcements and equipment. By the beginning of March 1941 the 5th Light Division also was receiving the remarkable 88mm artillery pieces. Originally these were designed as anti-aircraft guns, but proved to be lethal in an anti-tank role. It gave them the ability to knock out the heavily armoured British tanks like the Matilda. The 5th was the lead element in a major offensive that was launched on 31 March 1941. They were supported by four Italian divisions. Incredibly they managed to push the British back 600 miles.

The German and Italian units managed to capture both the British commander in Cyrenaica and his predecessor. Lieutenant General Philip Neame and Lieutenant General O'Connor were captured by a German patrol. Neame had been awarded the Victoria Cross when he was a lieutenant in the Royal Engineers at Neuve Chapelle on 19 December 1914. Luckily for the Germans and the Italians it was not the British 7th Armoured Division that they faced in Cyrenaica, but the newly created 2nd Armoured Division. The 7th had been withdrawn to Egypt due to the fact that they had very few serviceable tanks left.

Obviously such an enormous gain of ground required supplies and troops to be brought up from the key port of Tripoli. This collection of photographs shows knocked out vehicles and the progress of trucks along the main coast road.

This is a Matilda tank, or more specifically the Mark II, which was also designated the A12. It was designed as an infantry tank. The British had wanted a larger tank and it was developed out of designs that had begun in the late-1920s. The tank weighed around 27tons. One of its big problems was that initially there was no high explosive shell for the gun, so it had to use its machine guns for close support when working with infantry. It was considerably better armoured than even the German Panzer IIIs and IVs of its time. It had a distinctive cast turret and it was nicknamed *The Queen of the Desert*. When the Germans and Italians first encountered the vehicle they found it almost impossible to knock out. The armour was simply too thick for the standard Italian 47mm gun and shells fired from either German 37mm or 50mm anti-tank guns simply bounced off. It was, however, vulnerable to German 75mm and 88mm guns. Although it had good protection it was incredibly slow and could manage around 6mph in the desert. The suspension was not entirely reliable, it was underpowered and if it needed to undergo repairs this took an inordinate amount of time. Just less than 3,000 of the tanks were produced and the last vehicles were delivered in August 1943. It had proved quite difficult to manufacture, particularly the turret and the fact that it had a somewhat complicated suspension system.

This is a shot taken from one of the trucks, showing a knocked out British armoured car, probably a Marmon-Herrington, close to the roadside. This armoured car was based on a 3ton Ford truck chassis. Essentially it was a South African vehicle, as they had begun development in 1938. The South Africans used around 4,500 of them over the course of the war. In the desert the British also used the armoured car and they were fitted with a light machine gun and an anti-tank rifle. They were primarily used for reconnaissance. The vehicle was incredibly reliable, but it had poor armour. What is significant about the vehicle is that it was highly adaptable; over the course of the war many of them were modified and some could be seen with a British 2pdr anti-tank gun, Italian 20mm or 47mm guns, French 25mm guns or German 37mm guns. All of these adaptations meant that the turret had to be removed and the only thing to protect the gun crew was the gun shield. The armoured car was widely used, not only for reconnaissance but also as a command car and an artillery observation post. The Germans and Italians were also happy to use captured versions of this vehicle.

This is a Panzer II moving at speed across the desert. The Panzer II was something of a stop-gap tank and it was used extensively both in Poland in 1939 and in France in 1940. It had a relatively short front line service, as it ceased to be used by combat units by the end of 1942 and production ceased in 1943. In 1940 it was the most numerous type of German tank. This was really its high point, as it was relegated soon after to a reconnaissance role. Panzer IIs sent to North Africa had been modified so that they had a ventilation and filtering system, making them able to operate in the dry and dusty climate. When the 5th Light Division was deployed to North Africa it had forty-five Panzer IIs. It was also equipped with twenty-five Panzer Is, seventy-five Panzer IIIs and twenty Panzer IVs. In North Africa the Panzer II stayed in service throughout 1941, but by August 1942 there were just fourteen left. They were not replaced and we must assume that they had either been knocked out or been shipped back to Germany. Many of the chassis were actually used to build self-propelled guns, notably the Howitzer carrying Wespe.

Trucks are parked in the desert in this photograph. We can see that the area is deeply rutted with tyre tracks and that some trucks are parked on a ridge line in the background. As the German initial offensive developed the Australian 9th Infantry Division dug in at Tobruk. The bulk of the rest of the British and Commonwealth forces fell back to the Egyptian border. Tobruk was besieged but other German and Italian units pressed on to the east and recaptured Bardia and Fort Capuzzo. They then crossed the Egyptian border and took Sollum and Halfaya Pass. Tobruk was cut off and had to rely on resupply from the Royal Navy. Rommel's forces attempted to take Tobruk and it would prove to be a major thorn in his side. Without being able to take Tobruk it meant that trucks such as these had to make the long journey to and from Tripoli to bring up supplies. Had Tobruk fallen the supply line would have been cut significantly. It also meant that Rommel was hamstrung in his ability to build up his forces at Sollum to push deeper into Egypt.

This is a German tent *(zelt)* surrounded by supplies and equipment. This tent does not however appear to conform to any of the standard German issue tents. Superficially it is rather like a British issue conical tent, particularly on account of the open flaps at the top. It would not have been unlikely for German units to make use of captured British equipment. In fact any vehicles or equipment left behind by British and Commonwealth troops was routinely hunted through, particularly for tasty morsels. German troops in the desert were particularly fond of British and Commonwealth rations, cigarettes and Primus stoves.

A column of German trucks are proceeding along a track in North Africa here. Note the fuel or water bowser. In many other theatres of the war a high percentage of the fuel was not actually transported in tankers, but in canisters on regular trucks. Typically these cargo trucks would be used to carry jerry cans. Luftwaffe bowsers had a distinctive hump on the top of the tank, so it would appear from the photograph that these are not Luftwaffe. The likelihood is that these are in fact Opel Blitz fuel trucks, which were used by both the army and the Luftwaffe. The most common was the Opel Blitz bowser KFZ385. The bowser itself was known as a Flugbetriebsstoff-Kesselwagen.

Trucks have halted on fairly firm ground in this shot, on a track in the desert. The Germans developed a very efficient supply system in North Africa. Captured prisoners of war and German documents relating to the German 21st Armoured Division suggested that to supply the division there was a supply company and twelve supply columns. Of the twelve supply columns four of them were designated as heavy. Each had twenty-four vehicles, capable of carrying around 60tons of supplies. There were seven light columns, each with twelve vehicles and each of these could carry up to 30tons. The final column was for fuel and oil. The supply company was usually a labour company, with a strength of between 200 and 250 men. The labour company would cooperate with the supply columns to help unload, establish supply dumps and carry out maintenance. A division such as the 21st would have three supply dumps, which were relatively close together. The operating radius of the supply columns and the supply company was usually between 60 and 120 miles.

The German vehicle tactical symbol on this motorcycle combination designates it as belonging to a transport column or truck column. It is unlikely that this is a BMW R75, as unless this was a brand new delivery they were not distributed in any numbers until 1941. The BMW that was used in Africa led to some changes that saw metal fork covers being changed to rubber ones and an improved design, which incorporated an air filter located further up the motorcycle to keep it away from dust from the roads and tracks. This is likely, therefore, to be a Zundapp motorcycle. From 1940 around 18,000 of them were made. This was the KKS750 version. Zundapp had begun manufacturing detonators back in 1917 and had begun producing motorcycles shortly after the First World War. The first Zundapp was produced in 1921. Their heavy motorcycles, such as this one, began production in 1933.

This appears to be another captured British photograph. It seems to depict the same unit as the other captured photographs. Unfortunately the size and resolution of the photograph does not allow us to identify the precise unit in question. This photograph does not appear to have been taken in North Africa. It almost certainly depicts the British unit during the last stages of training before deployment. It is also clear that the destination of the unit had already been decided as they are kitted out in the early tropical kit that we have seen in the other photographs. Note the fact that the footwear appears to be ammunition boots with puttees.

This truck appears to have been caught in mud and is being dug out by one of the drivers. He is wearing an enlisted man's tropical visor cap, known as an afrikamützе. This is the head gear that is synonymous with the Afrika Korps. In actual fact it was used by a wide variety of German troops across the whole of the Mediterranean and the Aegean and also used by troops deployed around the Black Sea. When new it was an olive green to olive brown, although clearly it faded with continual use and sunlight. The man is not using the famous German foldable spade to dig out the truck. It would appear that he is using a full size infantry entrenching spade. It would have had a square nose. These were usually given out to infantry and artillery units and they would have been routinely strapped to the side of the trucks. They were slightly less than 5ft long. The spade tended to be narrow with straight sides and a straight front edge. They were designed to dig out soil that was compacted and needed to be cut through. The shovel in this photograph has a broader blade and has a rounded or semi-pointed tip and it was used to move looser material.

This photograph has the caption *Italian soldiers*. These Italian soldiers are wearing uniforms that were introduced in 1933. None of them are wearing their tunic but we can see their cotton shirts, which were of a pullover variety with the neck closed by small buttons. The collar had three points, two to the front and one in the back in the middle of the collar. They are wearing pantaloni, or breeches-style trousers. The leg is tied just under the knee. They were worn baggy and had a pair of slash front pockets and a rear slash pocket. They wore mollettiere, or puttees. Like the rest of the uniform they were of a khaki colour. They were wool strips that were cut so that they could be wrapped around the calf. Italian soldiers needed to be quite proficient at this, as the puttees had a tendency to unwind. The men are also wearing M1912 ankle boots that were laced and had a heel and toe cap. Generally troops in North Africa would wear natural brown boots. The socks underneath were quite unusual; the toes were left uncovered and there was a strap between the big and second toe that held the sock in place. The men were given a small, square cloth, which was to be folded over the toes to cover them. The men are wearing undress M35 bustina caps. They were of an envelope design with a front peak and ear flaps.

Trucks are descending down a road on the edge of an escarpment in this photograph. German truck production actually increased as the war continued. They managed to produce around 50,000 in 1941. This rose to 68,000 in 1943 and was slightly more the following year. As the war proceeded Allied bombing did hamper truck production. Bizarrely, Opel was actually owned by the American General Motors Corporation. GM was one of America's main producers of military equipment, but at the same time Opel in Germany was a key contributor to producing trucks and many key components for other vehicles and aircraft. The company in Germany also made use of slave labour, which posed GM with a considerable moral dilemma in the post-war years. Opel had not been performing that well as far as GM was concerned in the 1930s, but of course with the importance of wartime production the company had remained active and was making huge profits.

An unnamed location, probably in Libya, can be seen here, showing a military camp close to an Italian colonist settlement. Note the number of trucks moving about in the background. This area must have been set up as a supply base. The campaign in North Africa, or the western desert, was incredibly reliant on supplies and transport. Lack of supplies had been the reason behind Graziani's decision not to push forward further into Egypt in 1940. Key port supply bases proved to be essential during the campaign. Locations such as Tobruk and Benghazi were paramount and proved to be incredibly important, both for the Germans and for the British and Commonwealth forces. The North African campaign has often been described as being the quartermaster's nightmare. Both Rommel and later Montgomery were both reluctant to move in significant force before they had built up their resources. No attack was really possible unless their troops were properly prepared and supplied. The loss of supply bases, such as the one pictured, would have proved to have been disastrous.

This is a close up of one of the trucks on a tarmac road in Libya. We can clearly see the Afrika Korps palm tree and swastika insignia on the driver's side door. In March 1937 Mussolini paid a state visit to Italian Libya to officially open the Libyan coastal highway. It was renamed the Via Balbia after the governor general, Italo Balbo. He had died at the end of June 1940. After being an early member of the Italian Fascist Party and the Secretary of State for Air, Balbo became the Governor General of Libya in 1933. The centre of the road at the border between Tripolitania and Cyrenaica was marked with a marble arch called the Arch of Fileni. The arch was demolished in 1970 and on it was a motto that praised the greatness of the city of Rome. The Germans, Italians and the British and Commonwealth made full use of the road during the Second World War. There was heavy fighting on and around it and many of the damaged sections remained in a poor state for a number of years. It again saw combat in 2011, during the civil war that saw the ultimate overthrow of the Gaddafi regime.

This is a photograph of Leptis Magna. Undoubtedly this was the jewel in the crown of Roman Libya. The photograph shows the forum of Septimius Severus. The site itself is some 81 miles from Tripoli and it is now recognized as a World Heritage Site. In 2011 there was considerable fighting near the ruins and the Gaddafi regime was accused of hiding military equipment amongst the Roman site. Leptis Magna was originally a Phoenician city port. It fell into the hands of the Romans in 146BC. It gained its status in 193BC, as it was the birth place of the Emperor Septimius Severus. He used his position as emperor to turn Leptis Magna into one of the most magnificent and important cities in Africa. It is undoubtedly the most well preserved ancient Roman city in the Mediterranean.

In all likelihood this photograph is of Benghazi. There are a large number of sunken ships in the harbour. The British had been bombing Benghazi almost on a nightly basis between June 1940 and February 1941. Australians occupied it during the Operation *Compass* offensive, but then two months later the Afrika Korps took it back and Benghazi came under aircraft attack from the RAF once again. In December 1941 the British took it back and then Rommel seized the city once again, holding on to it for a year. After the defeat of Rommel at El Alamein, Benghazi was finally liberated on 20 November 1942. Understandably, after being subject to almost continuous attack for thirty months and having changed hands five times, the city was a mess. Most of the old Arab quarter, however, had actually escaped devastation, but the port area had been hit very badly and there were large numbers of wrecked ships in the harbour.

Chapter 3

Life on the Road

Whilst there were no special requirements for men that served in the Afrika Korps, they were required to undergo an additional medical and obtain a medical certificate of fitness for tropical service. This test, however, was not universal, as men were needed in Africa immediately and in any case even the efficiency of the German army failed in being able to process these men at short notice.

Each of the men would also receive an inoculation against both typhus and cholera. As we will see in this set of photographs, regular medical examinations were required, as were booster injections.

In almost any theatre of the Second World War, certainly as the war progressed, the standardized uniform of the German soldier broke down and men would wear a wide variety of different kit. Initially, standardized equipment was also the norm for the Afrika Korps and, perhaps, more important than anywhere else, the range of equipment had to be extensive to cope with the hot, airless days and the plunging temperatures at night. Hence men would be issued with daytime kit and equipment, such as shorts or tinted, anti-glare goggles, whilst at the same time they would have been given tropical greatcoats. The men would take a considerable amount of time to get used to the new conditions in North Africa. On the one hand they would have to cope with the blazing sun, but then prepare themselves for freezing cold nights.

As the campaign progressed and the supply situation worsened finding replacement equipment was nearly impossible and the men would make do and mend. They would not be averse to using British or Commonwealth equipment or supplies.

Each rank and file member of the Afrika Korps received an additional 2 Reich marks per day as their overseas allowance. Officers received an extra Reich mark each day.

Inside a vehicle in the heat of the desert the men would be subjected to extreme temperatures. They would also be constantly harassed by thousands of flies. As we will also see in this set of photographs, the men had to be pretty much self-sufficient, particularly when on the move. They could not necessarily rely on an efficient ration system.

Food spoiled very quickly and whilst the Germans' counterparts operating in Europe would have a diet that always included bread, butter and potatoes, in Africa this became black bread, dried beans and olive oil. Due to the proximity of Italy and the existing Italian infrastructure in North Africa, much of the Afrika Korps rations were in fact supplied by the Italians. Perhaps the most unpopular food was an Italian tinned, preserved meat. The tin was stamped with 'Administrazione Militare'. The prominent AM led to the soldiers, as in any army, coming up with alternative names for the contents. The Italians were apt to call it 'Arabio Morte', which roughly translates as 'Dead Arab'. Under their breath the Italians would also call it 'Asinus

Mussolini', the translation of which we will leave to the imagination of the readers. It is obvious that the tinned meat did not have that many fans either in the German or Italian armies. The Afrika Korps men were delighted if they could find British bully beef. They also loved British and Commonwealth hard tack biscuits and jams. If there was the possibility of getting hold of fresh meat, usually in the form of a stray goat, this was eagerly seized upon.

Both of the men in this photograph are wearing high tropical boots. They had brown leather around the feet and were originally a blue/grey or olive green that would fade over time to a very light tan. The uppers were canvas, with a brown leather liner. They were hobnailed and had eyelets for the lace up to the sixth pair of holes and then hooks for the remaining eleven fastenings. The Luftwaffe would have worn something similar, but these were usually in a tan canvas and had a flap over most of the fastenings above the ankle. This was secured by two buckled straps, presumably so that the lace, if it came loose, did not become snagged inside the aircraft. Officially these boots were designated as M1940 tropical high boots. They would have been issued particularly to the first groups of men that were sent over to Africa. As we will see in other photographs in this group, the high leather and canvas lace-up boots and the pith helmet were not that popular with the men. As time went on they would be much happier to replace their boots with something rather more practical.

In this photograph we can only hope that the jerry cans contain water rather than fuel. This man is receiving a haircut and more specifically his hair is being shaved off at ear level. The jerry cans were ubiquitous in the desert. The jerry can is actually a nickname given to the vessel by the British. It was designed to carry 4.5 gallons of liquid. In this make-do-and-mend theatre the British were delighted if they could get their hands on some of these German containers, as they proved to be far more resilient than their own petrol cans. The jerry can was used for water, fuel and oil. Note the jerry cans in the photograph are marked with a white cross. This was a universally adopted system, as it showed that the jerry can was only for water. Clearly it would have been disastrous to try to store water in a can tainted either by fuel or lubricants.

The men are fixing an engine problem in the desert in this photograph. The majority of German vehicles used in North Africa were painted either dark yellow or a sandy yellow. Some would often have a red/brown over the dark yellow or even dark green over grey. There was no real standardized system until at least 1942, at which point the vehicles were given a dark yellow coat of paint with a reddish brown camouflage or disruptive pattern. A year later this was changed to dark yellow alone.

Hanging out washing is the focus of this photograph. Part of the self-sufficiency also meant that it was only at supply bases, or main concentration points that the accepted infrastructure of the German army could be relied upon to carry out basic tasks, or even to supply replacement equipment. Whilst some of the men would be involved in servicing the vehicles at each stop, others would deal with water and fuel, whilst others cooked or others were engaged in laundry duty. Note this soldier has short tropical boots with socks folded over the top and the tropical sunhat.

Men are queuing up for inoculations in this shot. Sickness was the major cause of casualties, even compared to fairly heavy battle engagements during the North African campaign. At various stages during the campaign the numbers of men that had to be repatriated to Germany were greater than men making the reverse trip to replace them. Some of the biggest debilitating diseases were sand sores, dysentery, jaundice, a host of bowel complaints and diphtheria. Particularly when the units were static the diseases spread very quickly and medical supplies were also limited. Lice were a particular problem and Afrika Korps troops were not keen to occupy positions that had been previously manned by Italian units. They were believed to be infested with lice and fleas. German troops also tried to avoid desert Arabs for the same reason.

Clothes are being hand washed and this man seems to be paying particular attention to the seams, which could have been the hiding place for lice and fleas. Personal hygiene was incredibly important. Not only were there the lice and flea dangers, but also the fact that diseases would spread very easily. Due to the difficult supply situation a great deal of the medical supplies and medical staff were actually provided by the Italians. If men received a slight injury they would often stay with their unit, otherwise they would have to be evacuated to a field hospital. In instances where a wound or infection got too serious the men might be evacuated via Greece or Italy to Germany by air, or have to risk the more dangerous route back by hospital ship.

This man is focusing on the camera rather than the fact that the doctor is administering an inoculation. The Germans released a number of health pamphlets for their soldiers. They were issued by the German Army Surgeon General. Soldiers were expected to carry a copy of the pamphlet inside their pay book. It would give them basic advice on a wide variety of different issues. Most important was water. They were to never drink non-boiled water and not even use non-boiled water to clean their teeth. They were to avoid mineral water, lemonade and ice and they were even told not to bathe in streams, ponds or pools.

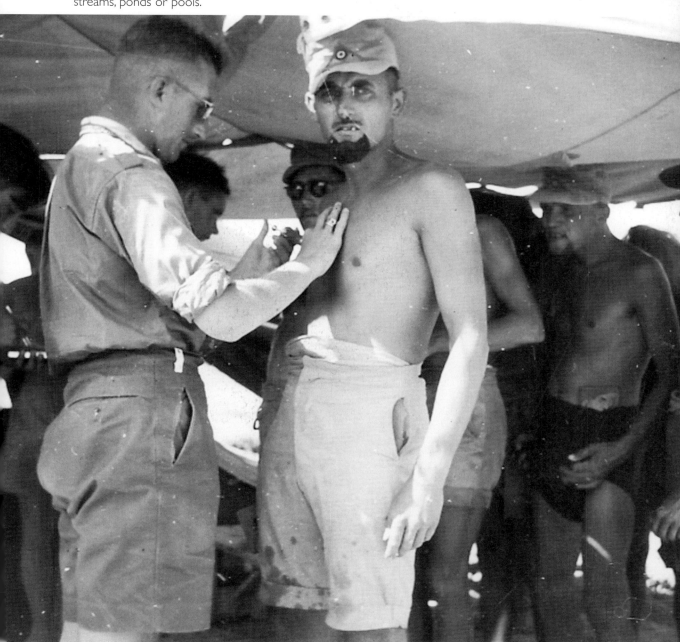

This is a typical shot of a member of the Afrika Korps. Note his decoration and the fact that he is wearing his field blouse over the top of a tropical issue, open-necked shirt. On duty the men were encouraged by the German Army Surgeon General to wear stomach bands. This was believed to prevent the men from catching a cold. They were told to wear their sun helmets during the hottest part of the day and, if this was not possible then they should wear their field caps. They were told always to wear their uniform and not to expose too much of their skin to the sun. They were also warned that excessive air temperatures would be particularly dangerous and they should reduce movement in these conditions if possible.

These men are having their boots inspected. Bizarrely, the inspecting officer is wearing a pair of native sandals and it would appear that the man presenting his boots is wearing a pair of gymnasium shoes. Note even at this relatively early stage of the war that there is a wide variety of different footwear. We can see the high leather and canvas tropical boots, ankle boots and other private footwear, presumably preferred by the soldiers whilst not on duty. Note that in the background there is also a dog. Pets were actively discouraged in the Afrika Korps. The men were told not to handle dogs, cats or monkeys for fear of rabies or worms or the risk of catching blood diseases.

This is a slightly blurred image of the men being shown the operation of a machine gun, which is mounted on a tripod. The machine gun nest is in the form of a rock sangar. This is an MG34, so-called because it came into service in 1934 and began to be issued in 1935. It was an air-cooled, general purpose machine gun. It could be fitted to a bipod and used as a light machine gun with a fifty-round ammunition belt in a drum, or, as in this case, on a larger tripod and belt-fed. It was originally designed by Heinrich Vollmer, based on a 1930s design that had been adopted by the Swiss.

This is a macabre photograph of a fallen British or Commonwealth soldier. We can clearly see his tin helmet. There are several knocked out trucks that appear to be of British design in the background. The first victory for Rommel in 1941 was at El Agheila. It was in fact a fairly minor engagement, even by North African standards. It was the point that the British had reached when they were forced to stop due to the fact that many of their units had been shipped out of the theatre to support the Greeks. This was the point at which Rommel and the Afrika Korps had the opportunity to launch their own offensive. They retook El Agheila in March 1941. Rommel would fortify the city and use it as a main base of operations and in fact after being beaten back during Operation *Crusader* in December 1941 it was at El Agheila that the Germans dug in and stopped the British offensive.

This photograph is captioned Georg Ottgen but unfortunately no trace can be found of this individual. It is not clear as to his unit, his rank or his fate. It was important for the men to quickly adapt to the different conditions that they would find in the North African desert. The country had entirely different customs, practices and religion. The men were routinely lectured about their nutrition, they were told never to eat raw meat or non-boiled milk. All fruit should be washed in purified water and peeled before eating and they had to be particularly careful not to buy from street vendors. The men were also told about flies, lice, ticks, snakes, mosquitoes and scorpions. They were supposed to use mosquito nets at night and carefully check that the insects had not got under the net or that there were any openings for them to get into.

This is a photograph of German and Italian shipping in the harbour of Tripoli. Tripoli and Benghazi were incredibly important as they were the main resupply ports for the Afrika Korps, as well as the Italian forces. The monthly capacity of Tripoli was around 45,000tons, although in times of emergency this could have been increased. Tripoli would have been able to manage around 1,500tons a day with Benghazi coping with slightly less than twice that. In the last three months of 1941 Italian and German shipping losses in the Mediterranean reached almost unsustainable levels. Not only that, but both ports were under almost continual attack from the RAF. This led to the loss of storage facilities, the sinking of smaller boats to help unloading and the vital trucks that were needed to transfer the supplies from the ports to the front line units. Both of the ports had relatively limited berthing facilities. Benghazi, for example, could handle two large vessels, a small vessel and one tanker at the same time.

This is the German cemetery at the White House, close to Tobruk. The graveyard is close to a German field hospital, which is in itself close to the Knightsbridge War Cemetery.

A number of well-kept German graves can be seen here, presumably at the same site. Note that the majority of the grave crosses have the men's tropical sunhats placed on them.

The stark reality for the local population was that their towns and villages were often subject to aircraft attack, shelling from artillery and, as in this case where a slip trench has been dug, ground fighting. Many of the population simply fled the major centres.

Trucks are moving in the desert in this photograph. The Germans used a wide variety of different road signs to direct their traffic. Drivers would have to keep their eyes open for important direction signs, but also for signs such as Wasser Ausgabe, which is roughly translated as a 'water supply'. Minefields, of course, were extremely common and they were marked with a skull and crossbones.

This photograph features an unidentified, presumably Italian-built town in Libya. Note the field car in the middle distance ahead of the truck column.

A German soldier can be seen here, who appears to be a military policeman. He is carrying a traffic signal in his hand and has his rifle slung across his back. He is wearing tinted goggles to protect his eyes. These men would have been a familiar sight for the truck drivers on the junctions close to supply dumps and military units.

This photograph was taken from the truck and it features a wrecked vehicle alongside the road. In the background it is possible to see several other vehicles. Two appear to be tanks and the third a truck. It is likely that these are also British and Commonwealth vehicles that have been abandoned or were knocked out in the early stages of the war in North Africa.

Another captured British photograph showing an unnamed unit. It is difficult to speculate when and where this photograph was taken. Given the fact that the photograph, along with others, fell into German hands, we must assume that the original photographs were either abandoned in a hasty retreat or were taken from British prisoners of war.

The whole truck company, with all of their officers, can be seen in this photograph in parade dress. They are posing in front of an unnamed barrack block, presumably in Germany. This photograph would have probably been taken in either 1939 or 1940.

Chapter 4

Nearing Tobruk

We have to assume that at this point, when this set of photographs was taken, Tobruk was still in the hands of British and Commonwealth troops. This was a dangerous part of the front for the trucks to pass. Not only were there increasing numbers of minefields, but also the area closest to the coast was under periodic bombardment from the Royal Navy. The trucks would also have received the unwelcome attention of RAF attacks, particularly on the main roads. As the trucks edged ever more eastwards the men would still have to cope with the day-to-day realities of desert life. Every time the men stopped they would attract flies. The flies would swarm over the men, hunting for moisture, and literally cover their food. This made daytime stops miserable. The men were supposed to have head nets, but these were in short supply. Eating was always a battle between the flies and the diner. It would be a constant challenge to eat the food without ingesting the flies that had attached themselves to the meal. As soon as the temperature began to drop the flies would become less of a problem, but as soon as the sun came up they would be there in their thousands. This would be particularly true if the men had not taken precautions when going to the toilet and buried whatever they had left in the desert.

This is a fascinating collection of photographs, as it illustrates the dangers that the truck drivers faced as they moved closer to the front on the Libyan/Egyptian border. What is particularly interesting is the number of wrecked aircraft and trucks along their route. Some of these aircraft are readily identifiable as Italian aircraft. Presumably these would have been casualties of the previous offensive, Operation *Compass*, which saw the Allies overrun the bulk of Italian held Libya.

As we will see in this set of photographs, this marks a definite point in the campaign. Tobruk was under siege by German and Italian forces, Rommel had pushed forward a battle group, which recaptured Fort Capuzzo and Bardia, both of which are featured within these photographs. The German troops had then pressed on to Sollum. This would have been the late spring of 1941. The next major operation was actually a fairly limited offensive. It was launched by the Allies and called Operation *Brevity*.

Operation *Brevity* was designed to strike German and Italian positions around Sollum. The operation was always seen as being a precursor for the much larger offensive, codenamed Operation *Battleaxe*. Both operations were conceived by General Archibald Wavell. He was the commander in chief of British Middle East Command.

Battleaxe was designed to take place in June 1941 and aimed to recapture Capuzzo, Sollum and the Halfaya Pass. The idea was to suck in as many of Rommel's tanks as possible and then, if circumstances allowed, to press on to relieve Tobruk.

To launch Operation *Brevity* Wavell had earmarked part of the 7th Armoured Division and the 22nd Guards Brigade. They were to be supported by the RAF. Facing them was the 2nd

Battalion of the 5th Panzer Regiment, a battalion of infantry of the Italian Trento Division and some Italian motorized infantry and artillery. The Allied centre column attacked the Halfaya Pass and other units managed to eventually overrun Fort Capuzzo. As the units probed to the west they came across increased resistance from German and Italian forces. Progress was relatively slow on the desert flank and on the coastal road the British were held up by determined Italian defensive positions. Eventually these positions were overrun and a number of prisoners taken.

Rommel believed that the attack he was facing involved far more tanks than was actually the case. Nonetheless he decided to counterattack. Capuzzo was recaptured and with the British forward units exposed they began a withdrawal. Operation *Brevity* had largely failed, but Halfaya Pass had been taken.

This photograph features a German soldier in his tropical greatcoat, eating from his mess tin. Many of the men were more active during the night than they were during the day. Certainly the evening was an ideal time to dig slip trenches, carry out patrols or resupply. Most strenuous activity took place in the evenings. The desert was often either extremely hot or extremely cold. In the early morning, which is presumably when this photograph was taken, the men were bundled up with greatcoats, tunics and collars to protect their necks.

A German motorcycle combination is seen here alongside an Opel Blitz truck. Note the unusual bonnet mascot, which is a British tin helmet. Due to the weather conditions it was also often the case that battles were timed to take place in the early hours of the morning, as soon as the sun had come up. Gains could be made before the temperature rose to unbearable levels. It would also give the vehicles the maximum opportunity to perform before they inevitably overheated in the extreme temperatures. For truck drivers on the road driving in the blazing heat of the day would not have been a comfortable option. They would have broken camp before sunrise in the morning, driven as far as possible until just before noon and then set up camp in preparation for the next day's drive.

A motorcycle combination is proceeding along a dirt track in Libya in this shot. Not restricted to having to contend with flies and the dust, there was also something known as a 'ghibli'. This was a localized, violent sandstorm. As we will see in future photographs in this chapter, accidents were most likely in these particular conditions. All of a sudden a sandstorm would brew up and vehicles such as this motorcycle combination would find it impossible to make any headway. In any case the motorcyclist would be unable to breathe. The winds were so strong that they could knock over a truck. Suddenly the temperature would increase and compasses would be affected by the electrical disturbance and the radios would go dead.

This is an overturned truck, which may well have succumbed to a localized sandstorm. Note the jerry cans, some of which are clearly marked with a white cross, designating them as water carriers, whilst others appear to be fuel cans.

This would appear to be a towed bowser, which has overturned when the road has collapsed. The desert was crisscrossed with dried riverbeds, or wadis. When there was heavy rain these wadis would be swamped with water. As the wadis dried out the surface beneath the road would dry out, crumble and become weak and many trucks and other vehicles fell prey to these enormous potholes. This photograph is actually captioned 'accident at Tobruk'. The possibility is that the road either collapsed or that a mine went off, or perhaps a shell landed close to the road.

This is another shot of the same accident. This shows the depth of the hole into which the truck strayed and subsequently overturned. Note the liquid running out of the bottom of the bowser. It must be assumed that this is water rather than fuel, otherwise additional precautions would have to have been made.

This is another clear shot of the accident. It does actually appear that the truck towing the bowser has come off the road and has fallen into a wadi or culvert. Without heavy lifting gear it would prove to be incredibly difficult to right the bowser. It would seem that from the relaxed manner of the men in the photograph that they are awaiting a crane, or perhaps a tank, to help pull the bowser back onto its wheels.

This is the final shot of the accident and we can actually see the water container on the truck that was towing the bowser. It would appear that each of these water containers carried 5,000ltrs. It is also possible to see that the bowser's container has been ruptured and that the precious fluid is pouring into the gaping hole beneath the bowser.

This is the first of two photographs that appear to show the aftermath of the road accident that saw the bowser overturn. These men are carrying out metal work along the roadside and amending the chassis of the bowser. These relatively crude repairs were necessary in the absence of more sophisticated repair facilities.

This is a clearer shot of the work on the bowser. We can see that the chassis has been dismantled and that the metal work is being worked on using a blow torch.

This is a shot of an Opel Blitz. This was the real workhorse of the supply lines. The enormous distances involved in the North African campaign made logistical support a nightmare. Often advances were 200 to 400 miles. Under normal circumstances only a working railway network could have possibly supported such advances. Nonetheless, the trucks had to do all the work. To put things into perspective, around 1,600 trucks were needed to replace the equivalent of a 200 miles double track railway. The Germans did try to establish a railway to the east of Tobruk. They sent out three locomotives and rolling stock. This was in around August 1942, but in a relatively short period of time the trains and the rolling stock had been knocked out by the RAF.

This photograph shows men consulting maps and instructions on the roadside. From the very outset the German units that had been sent to North Africa were a mixed bag. Although the units were motorized, the first division, the 5th, was made up of several different units, which were originally designed as defensive troops. The 21st Panzer Division had originally been an infantry unit and was not well versed in armoured warfare. It was not originally envisioned that Rommel would launch a major offensive, but simply bleed the British and Commonwealth forces in North Africa in a series of holding actions. This could have all changed, of course, had the attack on Russia in the summer of 1941 been totally successful and knocked Russia out of the war.

This photograph is marked as being Bardia. There had been a major battle here between 3 and 5 January 1941. This was part of Operation *Compass*. Bardia was a strongly held Italian fortress in Libya. The capture of the fortress was given to the Australian 6th Division, under the command of Major General Iven Mackay. He managed to take the position by attacking it from the west, at its weakest point. Holes were blown in the barbed wire and the anti-tank ditch filled. This allowed Matildas belonging to the 7th Royal Tank Regiment to lead the storming of the fortress, which led to the capture of 8,500 Italian prisoners. By the time the German truck drivers had arrived at Bardia the place had been recaptured. The capture of Bardia by the Australians in January 1941 had immediately led to the capture of at least 36,000 Italians in the area, along with a huge amount of material. Australian killed and wounded did not exceed 500.

Trucks are on the desert at dusk in this photograph. It would appear that the vehicle in the foreground is a Steyr field car. It was a general purpose utility vehicle. This is probably a Steyr 1500, which was used as a light truck, a command vehicle or an infantry carrier. Some were also converted into ambulances. They were made predominantly in Austria, where 10,000 were constructed, although there was an additional plant in Germany that produced another 6,000.

This photograph was probably taken in Bardia. It is clear to see the damage to the buildings from the shelling by the Royal Navy and the bombs dropped by the RAF. The vehicle in the foreground could easily be a captured Chevrolet or Ford. The Germans always had difficulty in providing their troops with sufficient trucks and they often used captured equipment. A prime example was a German mountain unit that arrived in Tunisia at the beginning of January 1943. None of their trucks, which were being transported by ship, arrived so they used French Peugeots. In fact some 15,000 of these Peugeots were made for the German army.

Fort Capuzzo can be seen in this photograph. When Italy declared war on Britain in June 1940 it was almost immediately captured by the British 11th Hussars and part of the 1st Royal Tank Regiment. It was then recaptured by the 1st Blackshirt Division and then recaptured by the British as part of Operation *Compass*. Rommel captured it again on 12 April 1941. When Operation *Brevity* was launched the British took it back and held it from 15 to 16 May. It was then abandoned and reoccupied by the Germans and Italians. It fell to the New Zealand Division as part of Operation *Crusader* on 22 November 1941. It once again fell to the Germans and Italians as part of the Battle of Gazala, which took place between 26 May and 21 June 1942. It finally fell to the British in the immediate aftermath of the second Battle of El Alamein, which took place between 23 October and 4 November 1942.

This photograph shows men enjoying an open air bath in the desert. We can only surmise that the two bathers only have an inch or two of water in the bath and can only begin to speculate where they found this bath.

This photograph is captioned 'fahrzeug appel', which roughly translates to mean 'vehicle inspection'. Checking the roadworthiness and general maintenance of a vehicle was a constant preoccupation. A truck breakdown in the middle of the desert would not only expose the men to unnecessary environmental dangers, but they could also be more easily spotted by enemy aircraft and would be sitting ducks. What is particularly interesting about this shot is that the awning on the truck appears to have Italian writing on it, which due to the angle of the shot and the sun is difficult to read.

Here we see a group of truck drivers admiring a German motorcycle combination. In 1941 the BMW R75 came into service and in 1942 a reconnaissance battalion was created for the Afrika Korps, which comprised of motorcycle combinations and Kubelwagens. This particular motorcycle combination is an earlier version and would have been used primarily to carry messages backwards and forwards. One man who used these motorcycle combinations on a regular basis was Hans Klein. He was a member of the Herman Goering Division and arrived in North Africa towards the end of 1942. Three or four times a week he would have to carry messages from headquarters in Tunis to other units. On one occasion his motorcycle was destroyed when it was hit by a British artillery bombardment. Luckily for Klein he was safely hidden in a foxhole.

These men are carrying out an inventory of spare parts and equipment. We can see that the equipment has been laid out on a corrugated sheet, held up by four water jerry cans. Amongst the equipment are numerous funnels, cables, tyre inner tubes and storm lanterns. Some of the other items are far more difficult to identify from the photograph.

These men are carrying out repairs to one of the trucks. Speed was always vital in the desert, primarily due to the lack of cover. All trucks would be susceptible to the effects of the sand and motorcycles in particular, due to the fact that their engine was exposed. This would mean that the machine could easily be disabled and the vehicle would have to be thoroughly cleaned before it would start again. Nothing could be wasted and everything had to be mended. Often broken parts would have to be repaired due to the short supply of replacements.

This photograph shows the men filling up water tanks from containers that have been elevated from the ground and camouflaged. Water was such a precious resource and arguably it was as important, if not more so, than fuel. Supplies of food, water and ammunition were never adequate. It was routine for the men to only have 2ltrs of water per day, rather than the recommended 4ltrs. This did not leave a great deal of water left over for washing. This was usually a luxury if the men were close to the Mediterranean coastline. The tremendous heat of the desert placed enormous strains on all of the soldiers and it was not unknown for men to pass out due to the heat.

Here we have a fascinating shot of an oasis, with numerous German trucks hidden amongst the palm trees. Water was often saved after washing and then filtered through a sand bucket, in order to wash clothes. It could then be filtered once again and used for showers. The men would often punch holes in cake tins and mount this on the side of a truck. One of the men would pour water into the cake tin whilst another stood underneath it and enjoyed the brief shower.

This is a closer shot of the oasis and the water cistern. In 1943 the Americans produced a report which investigated the water supplies for a typical German Panzer battalion in North Africa. Presumably the data was collected from captured German documents. The tank battalion, which is actually not named, left Tripoli for El Agheila with sufficient water for three days travel: 440 jerry cans were assigned for the cooling of engines and 450 for washing. The containers were distributed across all of the vehicles; medium tanks carried three and half-tracks and other vehicles two each. Each of the four companies carried 130 containers for cooking. Two gallons were assigned to each man for drinking purposes, so in total, over the three day period, nearly 12,000 gallons were required.

This is another close up of the elevated water storage containers. The men are filling jerry cans using a hose. There were several oases across Libya and one of the most famous is the Siwa Oasis, to the west of Qattara. Oases are formed by underground rivers or aquifers. This particular oasis appears to be a manmade well, which has allowed the water to reach the surface.

This photograph illustrates the process of the transferral of water from the truck into the jerry cans. During the whole of the North African campaign neither the Germans nor the Italians had particularly specialized forms of transport vehicles. The desert itself, providing the trucks stuck to trails, could easily be traversed. However, there was a huge amount of strain on shock absorbers and other key parts of the vehicle. Low-pressure balloon tyres were used and it was found that two tyres did not work because pebbles became wedged between the walls of the tyres. Air-cooled engines did not arrive in the North African campaign until pretty close to the conclusion in 1943, so there was no chance to really test them. Interestingly, the British Ford had better suspension than the German-built Ford and, wherever possible, spare parts from the British version were preferred. The vehicles all had shovels, planks and brush mats to help them get out of the sand if they became bogged down. Each truck had its own compass, which was placed in the cab so that it could be seen at all times.

This is a downed Italian aircraft, which appears to be a Fiat G50. It was all metal, with the control surfaces being fabric covered. Just less than 800 of the aircraft were built. The G50 first saw service in its pre-production guise during the Spanish Civil War. Subsequently they went on to be used in southern France. This aircraft was the first Italian single-seat all-metal aircraft. Twenty seven of them had arrived in Libya at the end of December 1940 and they flew their first combat mission on 9 January 1941. One G50 was lost when it was attacked by a Hawker Hurricane.

This shot shows a major explosion in the desert, which may have been caused by one of the trucks hitting a mine or the effects of enemy artillery or aircraft. Mines played an incredibly important role in the North African campaign. To put things into perspective, the Germans alone laid 80,000 mines in one line in Libya, at Buerat. In the post-war period it was estimated that just less than 20 million mines had been laid even as late as 1997 over 8,000 Egyptians were either killed or wounded as a result of the millions of mines that still are being found, either in Egypt or in Libya.

Here we see a burning truck. We know from work carried out by the British GHQ Middle East Tank Directorate that even in the early war period around 10 per cent of all British tanks were being knocked out by mines. The stark reality was that if a vehicle hit a mine there was a high probability that the driver and anyone else onboard would be killed. Comparatively speaking, mines gave individuals the greatest chance of survival. The British estimated that if a tank or vehicle was hit by an anti-tank gun then 40 per cent of the crew would either be killed or wounded. This rose to nearly 50 per cent if hit by a shell but just over 20 per cent if the vehicle rolled over a mine.

Several German aircraft can be seen on this airstrip. In the foreground is the Ju52, and in the background can be seen some Italian aircraft. The Ju52 was a real workhorse and known as either Iron Annie or Auntie Ju. It was manufactured between 1932 and 1945. In its military role it was primarily a troop and cargo transport aircraft. It would also have been used to evacuate seriously wounded troops back to Germany. It was a tri-motor aircraft and one of its most famous uses was as an aircraft for paratroopers or to tow gliders and was used extensively in Holland and then for the Battle of Crete. It was estimated that 280 Ju52s were lost in Holland alone. It was a slow and ponderous aircraft, so it was quite susceptible to anti-aircraft fire and it could only fly half the speed of a Spitfire. In North Africa a large number of Ju52s were lost on what has become known as the Palm Sunday Massacre. This took place on 18 April 1943. A dozen Spitfires belonging to RAF Squadron No 92 and nearly fifty USAAF P-40s encountered a formation of Ju52s over Tunisia. An enormous number of the Ju52s were lost in the ensuing dogfights.

This photograph shows the gutted remains of a spotter aircraft. The Germans used the Fieseler Storch, which was used throughout Europe and North Africa. The Storch is perhaps best known for its involvement in the rescue of Mussolini from Gran Sasso and as the last aircraft to land in Berlin on 26 April 1945. The British, on the other hand, used the Auster as a military liaison and observation aircraft.

This is a truck burning in the distance. Note the scattered deployment of trucks in the foreground. Many of the men that had been rushed to Africa at very short notice had received very little instruction about the types of conditions that they would encounter. As a result the Germans instituted a series of lectures and exercises, amongst which was how to travel over extensive areas of sandy terrain and how to cover and camouflage themselves in open terrain. The men would also practice night driving and orientation by compass and by the stars. They would also be instructed as to how to recover vehicles in sandy terrain. To improve the efficiency, changes were brought into effect towards the end of 1941. Special units, including water supply companies and water transport columns with geological teams were established in order to ensure a regular water supply and to deal with the growing transportation problems. All of the vehicles were camouflaged by a coat of desert coloured paint. Men were also given a broader range of equipment and clothing.

This is an unidentified aircraft which is passing over the truck column. Throughout the North African campaign German units found themselves exposed to the RAF, who were extremely active. They were to experience attacks on an almost daily basis. To begin with the Germans suffered large losses as a result of allowing their trucks to bunch up. Over the weeks the men learned to disperse their units, both in breadth and depth. It was suggested that the minimum distance between the vehicles should be at least 50 yards, if not 100. The truck drivers were told to dig in if they were to halt for any period of time. This included the trucks. They were expected to dig trenches for the vehicles so that they would at least protect the axles from bomb fragments. This would, of course, also have helped to protect the tyres. Camouflage nets were to be used if possible and every man was to dig his own fox-hole.

This photograph shows the wrecked remains of what is believed to be an Italian bomber in the foreground. Behind the wreck are at least two German Stuka dive bombers. The Ju87, or Stuka, was specifically adapted for use in North Africa. This was known as the Ju87B-2/Trop. It had sand filters and a desert survival kit. The Ju87 was initially very successful in North Africa; however as British air power in the theatre improved the Stuka was easy prey. In 1941 most Ju87 operations in North Africa were focused on the siege of Tobruk, which was to last some seven months. The Stuka also was present at the battles of Gazala and both of the battles of El Alamein. By the autumn of 1942 Stuka losses in North Africa had reached crippling levels. By the time the Allied forces landed in North Africa for Operation *Torch* the Stuka was effectively obsolete and on one day, 11 November 1942, fifteen of them were shot down in a matter of minutes by USAAF Curtiss P-40s.

Passing an abandoned spotter aircraft that has been left near the roadside. If truck and other vehicle drivers had problems with the sand then this was an even greater hazard for aircraft and their crews. Sand filters were attached to intake valves, but the engines still wore out quicker. Very fine dust particles were not blocked out by the air filters. It was particularly difficult to keep the dust away during refuelling. In dust storms it was almost impossible for the pilots to see and visibility could be as poor as 10 yards. Dust could remain hanging in the air for a long time, making take offs and landings very dangerous. On the other hand, the dust and the sand made it actually easier for pilots of observation aircraft. They could see absolutely everything moving on the ground. The trouble was that it often led to inexperienced spotters reporting that they had seen far bigger formations of enemy troops than actually existed.

This is a difficult aircraft to identify due to the angle and the quality of the photograph. It is also difficult to try to work out the markings on the aircraft at this scale. Aircraft crews were told to try for an emergency landing rather than bale out over the desert. It would make the aircraft and crew far easier to find. It was actually quite rare for German aircraft to be deployed in the interior. If a German aircraft landed even behind enemy lines they were told that the local Arabs were likely to be friendly and helpful and that the majority of them were sympathetic to the Germans. Distress signals consisted of smoke signals and signal ammunition, but these had to be used at the right moment if the crew could hear an aircraft overhead. Larger aircraft did carry emergency radio transmitters. The men were told to remain near the aircraft if possible.

A number of aircraft are flying over a desert camp in this photograph. It is believed that these are Italian transport aircraft. German pilots and crews were given special equipment for the desert. Each man was given 2ltrs of bottled water and they also had a small emergency ration pack. This consisted of hard sausage and biscuits, grape and sugar tablets, cognac and Coca-Cola. The crew was also given a gasoline stove and there were one-man tents, sleeping bags and rubber mattresses. The men also had storm matches, flashlights, sun reflectors and a first aid kit. For personal protection they were given a three-barrelled hunting gun and a hunting knife. They would have foreign currency and an emergency compass, as well as a signal pistol with ammunition. There was a special desert emergency search squadron, which consisted of around nine to twelve Fieseler Storch aircraft, as well as a number of personnel carriers that would extract the men once they had been spotted.

Chapter 5

Out and About in the Desert

German operations in North Africa had to be meticulously planned. The normal course of events would be to transport German troops, equipment and supplies by rail to Italian ports. The German and Italian ships would then be used to run the gauntlet across the Mediterranean into a North African port. The transportation responsibilities fell to a special branch known as Transportation to Africa. This organization fell under the control of the individual who had been the Military Attache in Rome. He was now operating as a full general and attached to Italian military headquarters.

Once the vessels had arrived in North Africa the troops, equipment and supplies then became the responsibility of the Supply and Administration Officer of the Afrika Korps. This title was later changed to Chief Supply and Administration Officer of the Panzergruppe. This was again later designated from Panzergruppe to Panzer Army of Afrika and then German-Italian Panzer Army.

Back in 1941 Field Marshal Kesselring was appointed as Commander of the German 2nd Air Force. He would be based in Italy and his primary responsibility was to use both Italian and German naval and air assets to protect the reinforcement and supply vessels heading for North Africa. He was also responsible for interdicting British transport operating in the Mediterranean. This job was vital, as all bulk requirements for North Africa were transported by sea. However it would later be the case that as the number of ships lost rose most personnel were transported to North Africa by aircraft.

Kesselring placed an emphasis on trying to protect German and Italian ships, rather than focusing on stopping the Allies from reinforcing their troops. As it was he had insufficient resources and had to make do and mend.

The primary responsibility for keeping open the shipping lanes fell to Italian Supreme Command. He knew that the supply services would collapse and therefore the effort in North Africa would fail if something could not be done. Immediately after his arrival for a short period of time, until May 1941, the supply situation improved to a great extent. Convoys were reaching Tripoli on a regular basis with very few losses. When Benghazi was captured this was also used as a major port.

Italian submarines were deployed from around April 1941 to bring in fuel to the lead elements of the Afrika Korps. They came in at the port of Derna. Kesselring also organized a flotilla of small boats to operate along the African coast.

By June 1941 the Allies had begun to deploy increasing numbers of Royal Navy submarine and surface vessels to prevent reinforcement and resupply. Losses mounted and tanks were now being transported using naval barges and men and equipment were being brought in by air. The RAF had made the use of Bardia almost impossible for the Germans.

By December it was decided that Italian battleships would now be used to protect the convoys heading to North Africa. For the first six months of 1942 the Germans had local air superiority across the shipping lanes. Kesselring had also ordered round-the-clock attacks on Malta, to prevent Allied aircraft based there from interfering. German losses dropped and this allowed Rommel to launch a new offensive. He managed to reach the Egyptian border. So good was the improvement that he actually had stockpiles of supplies to last him up to eight weeks.

By July 1942 the situation had become more complex. Dropping supplies off either at Tripoli or Benghazi meant that the men and materials had to be driven hundreds of miles to reach the new front. Aircraft were deployed by the Germans in Sicily, southern Italy and Greece. Malta had resurfaced as a major problem. The RAF had stationed bombers on the island and they were halting the German convoys. As 1942 continued the sea routes to the ports of Benghazi and Tripoli were cut.

Kesselring was forced to route supplies via Crete, but this was air transportation and could never meet the demands of the Afrika Korps. When the Germans occupied Tunis this reduced the distance that troops and equipment had to move across the Mediterranean, but this was at a time when Anglo-American forces had landed in North Africa and they had seized air superiority. It was almost impossible for any German or Italian vessel to make it unscathed across the Mediterranean.

With the British advancing out of Egypt and across Libya and the Anglo-American forces menacing the Germans from the west, North Africa effectively became cut off. There was no chance of any significant resupply. It would only be a matter of time before the remaining German and Italian forces in North Africa would be overwhelmed.

If the caption for this photograph is correct, this is the German heavy-lift ship, *Ankara*. This must put the photograph considerably before January 1943, as she was sunk by mines that were laid by HMS *Rorqual*. This submarine was a mine laying version that had been built in 1936. Her most famous role was her involvement in running supplies to Malta in 1941. She was under the command of Captain Lennox Napier who had been involved in submarine warfare since 1934. He took command of the *Rorqual* in June 1941. After the vessel's involvement in running supplies to Malta she returned to her normal duties of mine laying. In August 1942 they sank an Italian steamer. Later in the month they sank another merchant ship and survived a depth charge attack. In January 1943 the submarine laid a number of mines on the approaches to Tunis. The *Ankara* was carrying tanks for the Afrika Korps and she was lost when she hit the mines. *Rorqual* went on to sink the oil tanker *Wilhelmsburg*, which was carrying oil to Greece. She torpedoed the vessel in the Dardanelles approach. In total the *Rorqual* laid over 1,200 mines, the highest total for any British submarine. In 1945 she was sent to join the Royal Navy in the Pacific, but she was scrapped at Newport in 1946.

The caption for this photograph identifies this vessel as an Italian battleship in the port of Naples. Italian battleships were deployed to protect convoys heading for North Africa. Although this vessel is not specifically identified, it is a Littorio or Vittorio Veneto Class battleship belonging to the Italian Navy. There were only four of them, which were constructed between 1934 and 1942. They were the *Littorio*, the *Vittorio Veneto*, *Roma* and *Impero*. *Littorio* was torpedoed at Taranto in November 1940 and again in June 1942. The *Vittorio Veneto* was torpedoed in March 1941 and again in the September. *Roma* did not go into service until June 1943 and the *Impero*, still in an uncompleted state, was taken by the Germans in 1943 and used as a target ship.

This photograph is captioned as the 'leader of the flock'. It is an unidentified German merchant vessel, which is bound for North Africa. When vessels arrived in North Africa they would tend to be unloaded by local Arabs. The Germans simply lacked the manpower to do this themselves and found it incredibly difficult to encourage locals to continue to unload during RAF attacks. It was also difficult to continue the loading or unloading processes during the hottest hours of the day. In response to the reduced levels of supplies and equipment the Germans were forced to make good many of their losses by using captured equipment.

This is a photograph of three of the men who appear on a regular basis in this photograph album. They are standing alongside what is believed to be the *Ankara*. These men, although from an unidentified unit, certainly saw action or at least were posted in the Balkans and in Greece. At some point the unit would have made their way presumably to Naples for embarkation to North Africa. It is suspected that this would have been towards the end of 1941.

Members of the transport unit are lined up in front of their trucks and coaches with all of the equipment stowed. The men have all been issued with tropical helmets and are fully equipped with the long, German laced boots. Note the two individuals to the left front of the photograph who have large map cases attached to their belts. Presumably these are officers. The bulk of the rest of the men have ammunition pouches. Judging by the background, this photograph was probably taken in Naples before embarkation, rather than in North Africa.

This is a photograph that appears to have been posed on the slopes of Mount Vesuvius. Mount Vesuvius is a short distance (less than 6 miles) to the east of Naples. Although Vesuvius is, of course, well known for its part in the destruction of Pompeii, it has in fact erupted far more recently. In 1906 one hundred people were killed and the last major eruption was in March 1944. It destroyed three villages and badly damaged a fourth. Larva flows were prominent between 18 March and 23 March 1944. By that stage the USAAF's 340th Bombardment Group was in the immediate vicinity, occupying the airfield at Pompeii. The eruption caused damage to several of their B-25 Mitchell bombers and in fact as many as eighty-eight of them were so badly damaged that they had to be written off.

Onboard the *Ankara*. We can see a variety of German trucks and buses, along with what appears to be a towed wagon that would have served as a command post. Assuming this voyage took place in the brief period that the Germans and Italians controlled the shipping lanes from Italy to North Africa, the voyage would not have been very dangerous or noteworthy. The men certainly appear relaxed in this photograph.

As we could also see in the previous photograph, the men are wearing German lifejackets. These are not the type of lifejackets that were issued to either men of the Luftwaffe or the Fallschirmjager. They were of a more intricate design, with several more sausage-shaped individual cells. These lifejackets appear to be far cruder. There were various different styles of lifejacket. Each of them consisted of a number of air bladders. The ones shown in the photograph were also not the type used by the German navy, which were only inflated when they needed to be used.

This is an Italian general hospital, probably in Naples. A later photograph was taken by the US Army when the site became the 300th General Hospital. It would seem that the hospital complex in Naples had long been involved in dealing with battlefield casualties. It may be that this photograph was taken because the owner had a medical background, or his unit could have been involved in transporting wounded German and Italian troops. When it was being used by the Americans later in the Second World War the hospital was used to deal with serious injuries. One American soldier who belonged to the 143rd Regiment of the 36th Infantry Division was hit in the leg with shrapnel and had one of his fingers cut off. He was initially dealt with at a first-aid station and then spent forty-five days recovering from his wounds at this hospital. Unfortunately for the individual he had hoped that the wounds were bad enough for him to be sent home, but he found himself fighting in France and was also involved in crossing the Rhine with Patton's 3rd Army.

The photographer's unit is lined up, now in North Africa. The owner of the album is marked with a cross and he stands at the end of the front line. It is presumed that this photograph was taken in 1941, as the bulk of the men are wearing standardized uniforms and all have tropical hats.

A command car stops for a posed photograph on the outskirts of Benghazi here. Benghazi was a settlement that had existed before the Greeks and Romans and its appearance in the 1930s and 1940s owed a great deal to the Ottoman Turks and the Italians. The city had grown but due to its geographical position, being virtually at the centre of the North African campaign, it was inevitable that it would be the scene of fighting and persistent bombing. The damage caused to the city over some thirty months of fighting was massive. It had changed hands five times, its streets had been fought over and shells had been fired at it from the land and from the sea and it had been bombed on numerous occasions. The narrow streets of the Arab quarter seemed to have had a charmed existence, although many other areas of the city were devastated.

This photograph shows a roadside stop in Libya. These roads out of Benghazi were strategically important. On 25 March 1942 David Stirling, founder of the Special Air Service, launched a raid against Benghazi itself. Along with six other men they managed to get into the port and with them they had a fold-up canoe and a rucksack of limpet mines. Their plan was to attach them to Italian warships in the harbour. The canoe proved to be unseaworthy, so they called off the mission. A month later they tried again; it was a similar plan but this time they had two rubber dinghies. This also proved to be a failure because the dinghies had been punctured *en route* and they could not blow them up. In the hope of being third time lucky, they returned in the September, but this time they were ambushed and had to abandon the mission once again.

Local Arabs are prudently standing alongside the road here, as a German transport column passes them. It goes without saying that camels were a common sight in Libya. One Australian soldier, writing to his sister in 1941, recounted an altogether more sinister use of the camel. The Germans seemed to get into the habit of finding camels and then herding them towards the British lines. The idea was that the camels would trigger off landmines. The unnamed Australian unit was wise to this ruse and, under the cover of darkness, shot the three camels and dragged them back to their lines, where they skinned them, butchered them and enjoyed fresh meat for the next few days. Apparently it tasted like veal.

This is a photograph of a Ju52 taken from the window of another aircraft over the Mediterranean. Due to its slow speed, Ju52s were incredibly vulnerable. The RAF 272 Squadron, on 25 October 1942, engaged thirty-five Ju52s being escorted by half a dozen Me110s. Eight Beaufighters found the German aircraft to the north of Tobruk. Two of the Ju52s were shot down and later the same unit attacked El Adem airfield and destroyed another two Ju52s, shooting down a third as it came into land. The Ju52 was proving to be incredibly vulnerable, but as the seaborne supply line was strangled this became the only option for the Germans in North Africa.

A close up of one of the members of the unit is seen here, standing alongside a Ju52. The Ju52 had a peculiar look to it, with its low cantilever wings and its corrugated-metal skin, together with its tri-motor arrangement. The fuselage was rectangular, with a domed decking. We can just see the steps leading up to the port side passenger door, which is just aft of the wings. The undercarriage was fixed and it also had a tail skid (later a tail wheel). Originally the Ju52 was Hitler's personal transport aircraft but by September 1939 this had been replaced by a Focke-Wulf Fw200 Condor.

A German officer (probably the owner of this album) is standing alongside two Italian soldiers in this photograph. Judging from the colour of the soil and the vegetation this photograph may either have been taken in Italy, or in the coastal strip of Libya. The two Italians are carrying the Carcano bolt action rifle. This was a range of weapons that were produced between 1891 and 1945. Some of the rifles still remained in use until as late as the 1980s. In fact during the recent Libyan civil war a number of these rifles appear to have resurfaced and were used by the rebels. The range of rifles developed over the course of the 1930s and early 1940s, and many of them, were actually shipped to either Finland or Japan.

This photograph does appear to have been taken after the unit had been in Africa for some time. Note the variety of different clothing that the men are wearing and their more typical Afrika Korps appearance. All three men are wearing the tropical greatcoat, which was dated to around 1941. Strangely enough, many of the examples of these coats that still exist have a dominant PW stamped on the back, which was a US stamp for prisoners of war. These overcoats would have belonged to men that were captured in 1943 and, presumably, shipped to the United States for the duration of the war. Many of the men were subsequently returned to Europe via Britain for repatriation.

This photograph shows a memorial to the 5th Light Division, which was a motorized division and the first unit to be shipped over to North Africa as part of Rommel's new Afrika Korps. The 5th Light Division was a rather makeshift unit and consisted of the 5th Panzer Regiment and a motorized infantry regiment. It was supported by anti-aircraft units, a Panzerjager battalion, artillery, anti-tank and a reconnaissance battalion. Many of the units had been stripped out of the 3rd Panzer Division. It was called a light division as, compared to a Panzer division, it was not as heavy in terms of tanks.

The truck convoy comes to a halt on a desert road in Libya in this shot. On close inspection this appears to be an infantry transport unit. The most common pistol that was issued to German officers was the Walther P38. This can be seen in the holster of the man on the right-hand side of the photograph. It was a semi-automatic pistol, which was designed to replace the Luger. The P38 was in production between 1938 and 1963. Strangely, it was reintroduced to the German army in 1957 and until 1963 became their standard firearm.

A German motorcycle and sidecar are featured in this photograph, in rough Libyan terrain. The motorcycle did not prove to be very useful in the desert, as it was so prone to breakdown as a result of the sand and dust. This was all part of a learning curve for the German army and, as time went by, they began to adapt to conditions in the Western Desert and to the changing nature of warfare. To begin with, for example, the Germans had arrived in Africa with their 37mm anti-tank guns. These proved to be virtually useless against Matildas. By the summer of 1941 they were using 50mm anti-tank guns and then by the beginning of 1942, captured Russian 76.2mm anti-tank guns. As far as the motorcycle was concerned, by the beginning of 1942 large numbers of them had already been replaced with Kubelwagens. The Germans had tried to use the Kettenkrad, which was a half-tracked motorcycle, but this had proved to be completely unsatisfactory in the desert.

The caption of this photograph seems to suggest that the man on the right-hand side is an Italian, possibly from a blackshirt unit. There were 340,000 blackshirts by 1940. These were in three divisions; the 1st, 2nd and 4th and all of them were lost during the North African campaign. Essentially they were paramilitaries. The organization had been created in 1919 and originally consisted of some 200,000 men who took part in Mussolini's march to Rome in 1922. Essentially they became a volunteer militia force.

An SdKfz7 8ton half-track prime mover is featured in this photograph. Production had begun on this vehicle in 1933, but it was not put into mass production until 1939. Just more than 12,000 of them were produced and there were still more than 3,500 of them in service by the spring of 1945. The SdKfz7 was used to tow heavier artillery pieces, including 88mm flak guns. They could tow around 8,000kg and could also carry twelve men along with all of their ammunition and supplies. The vehicle had a range of around 156 miles on the road and 75 cross country. In its basic form, which we see here, it was 6.85m long, 2.6m high and 2.35m wide. The British captured some SdKfz7s in North Africa and they were so impressed by them that the Luton factory, belonging to Vauxhall Motors, were taken on to build a copy. This was known as the BT but only half a dozen of the prototypes were ever made.

Familiar German faces pose alongside some Libyan Arab children here. There is a complex tribal system in Libya and at least 140 different tribal groups. During the Italian occupation Libya was in fact split up into two different colonies: Cyrenaica and Tripolitania. The term Libya was not actually adopted until 1934. In the period 1928 to 1932 huge numbers of Bedouin were killed, either directly by the Italian military or as a result of starvation and disease. Over the period of the 1920s and 1930s around 150,000 Italians settled in Libya; this constituted around 20 per cent of the total population. The Italians, although driven out of Libya, did not actually relinquish formal control of the country until 1947.

The back of a German bus is featured in this photograph. It is possibly an Opel. This was a staff bus that was built on the chassis of the Opel Blitz. They were built in Essen between 1939 and 1943 and during this time around 3,000 of them were made. They were used for a variety of purposes, including officer transport, ambulances, telephone exchanges and radio vehicles.

This is another shot of a German motorcycle combination. From the tactical sign on the side of the motorcycle combination it would appear that this vehicle is attached to a workshop company. These men would have been responsible for all types of vehicle maintenance and repair. Each motorized unit and tank regiment was provided with a workshop company. A tank regiment, for example, would have a headquarters platoon, two repair platoons, a recovery platoon, an armoury section and workshops for communication equipment and, finally, a company supply section. In rest areas the repair unit would check to see if vehicles were serviceable. They would travel with their units and deal with any vehicle or equipment breakdown. The usual rule of thumb was that they would try and deal with it if the vehicle could be repaired in less than four hours, otherwise it would be towed away by the recovery platoon. These two men were probably repair crews. They were given a motorcycle and sidecar and would effectively have been the emergency service that would travel to the breakdown and assess the repair, carrying it out if possible.

This is a soldiers' home, or club, in Tripoli. Here the men could buy cigarettes, wine, beer, coffee, iced water and, if they were lucky, chocolate. It would appear that this particular canteen was named after General Rommel. The term 'soldatenheim' means 'military canteen'.

This photograph is marked as having been taken in Derna, or at least on the outskirts of it. Derna is in eastern Libya and was often used as an interrogation point for captured British and Commonwealth troops. The Germans had installed an informer, who was later identified as Private Theodore John William Schurch. He was accused of spying for the Germans when he came to trial in September 1945. He faced nine counts under the 1940 Treachery Act. He apparently went absent without leave in October 1942 and somehow offered his services to the enemy. Schurch was not British, but Swiss and had been a long-term spy of the Italians. He had joined the British Royal Army Service Corps as a driver. He was sentenced to death by hanging and was duly executed on 4 January 1946.

This is another shot of the docks, presumably taken in Tripoli. It was only from the ports of Benghazi and Tripoli that significant amounts of men, ammunition, fuel and other supplies could be moved. The Germans did look at trying to install a railway to the front, but this would have needed at least 60,000 tons of equipment, including the locomotives. The Germans did give it serious consideration; they calculated it would take twelve months to build the Tripoli to Benghazi section alone. At Tripoli most of the ammunition and fuel had to be stored in the open. There were very few shelters. The Germans were forced to disperse their supplies and ammunition over a relatively large area and then to camouflage them. Despite express orders to disperse this vital equipment, it was often ignored and, as a result, a large amount was lost due to bombing.

This would appear to be a German Krupp truck. These were produced from 1931 and around 2,000 of them were made. They were used by all arms of the German military until around 1942.

This is a fascinating photograph, which shows a huge variety of different vehicles stretched out along a road. We must assume that the Germans were confident of their air cover at this stage, otherwise the vehicles would have been parked much further apart and an attempt would have been made to camouflage them if this had been a night stop. We can see fuel tankers, standard trucks with lifting equipment and the towed command wagon, which we first saw on the ship bound from Naples to Tripoli. Whilst trucks may have been used in the desert certainly in the early stages of the war, it became increasingly the case that the Germans used tank chassis as their primary recovery vehicles. A huge variety of different chassis were used, including those from the Panzer III, IV, V and VI. In addition to this the Germans used captured T-34 chassis and the 38T, which was originally Czechoslovakian.

German soldiers are fraternizing with local Libyan children. One of the children is wearing the German sand goggles. There was a wide variety of different types of goggles used by the German troops in order to protect their eyes in the desert. Some of them were specifically tinted, whilst others were larger and primarily designed for motorcyclists. We can also see that the soldier on the right of the photograph has his dog tags around his neck. These were known as hundemarken. As would be expected, the dog tags would have a wide variety of different abbreviations on them. They would identify blood group, unit and army number.

Bibliography

Carell, Paul, *The Foxes of the Desert,* MacDonald, 1960

Coggins, Jack, *The Campaign for North Africa,* Doubleday, 1980

Lewin, Robin, *The Life and Death of the Afrika Korps,* Pen & Sword, 2003

Lewin, Robin, *Rommel as a Military Commander,* Pen & Sword, 2003

Lucas, James Sidney, *Panzer Army Africa,* Presido, 1978

Moorehead, Alan, *The Desert War, The North African Campaign 1940 to 43,* Hamish Hamilton, 1965

Strawson, John, *The Battle for North Africa,* Pen & Sword, 2004

Windrow, Martin, *Rommel's Desert Army,* Hippocrene, 1976